*Small Scale
Observations*

ALSO BY JAMES SUTHERLAND-SMITH

BOOKS AND PAMPHLETS

Four Poetry and Audience Poets P&A, Leeds 1971
A Poetry Quintet Gollancz, London 1976
The Death of Orpheus Words Etc., London 1976
Trapped Water Earthgrip, London 1977
Death of a Vixen Many Press, London 1978
A Singer from Sabiya Many Press, London 1979
Naming of the Arrow Salamander Imprint, London 1981
The Country of Rumour Many Press, London 1985
At the Skin Resort Arc Publications, Todmorden 1999
In the Country of Birds Carcanet, Manchester 2003
Popeye in Belgrade Carcanet, Manchester 2008
Mouth Shearsman Books, Bristol, 2014
The River and the Black Cat Shearsman Books, Bristol, 2018

TRANSLATIONS *(with Viera Sutherland-Smith except where stated)*

Not Waiting for Miracles Modrý Peter, Levoca 1993 (with Štefánia Allen and V S-S)
Slovensky balady Pavian Records, Bratislava 1995 (with Zuzanna Homolová)
Swallowing a Hair. Poems by Ján Ondruš, Studna, Bratislava 1998 (with Martin Solotruk)
An Album of Slovak Literature, Bratislava 2000
100 Years of Slovak Literature, Bratislava / Vilenica, Slovenia 2000
Cranberries in Ice: Selected Poems of Ivan Laučík Modrý Peter, Canada 2001
The Melancholy Hunter: Selected Poems of Ján Buzassy Modrý Peter, Canada 2001
Scent of the Unseen. Selected Poems of Mila Haugová Arc Publications, Todmorden 2002
And That's the Truth: Selected Poems of Milan Rúfus Bolchazy-Carducci Publishers,
    Mundelein, IL. 2005
Dinner with Fish and Mirrors: Selected Poems of Ivana Milankov Arc Publications,
    Todmorden, 2013 (with Zorica Pavičić)
Selected Poems of Miodrag Pavlović, Salt Publications, Cromer, 2014 (with Nenad Aleksić)
Tidal Events. Selected Poems of Mária Ferenčuhová, Shearsman Books, Bristol, 2018
The Other Monk. Selected Poems of Ján Gavura. F.A.C.E. Slovakia 2019 (with the author)
Eternal Traffic, Mila Haugová, Arc Publications, Todmorden, 2020

James Sutherland-Smith

Small Scale Observations

Shearsman Books

First published in the United Kingdom in 2022 by
Shearsman Books
P O Box 4239
Swindon
SN3 9FN

Shearsman Books Ltd Registered Office
30–31 St. James Place, Mangotsfield, Bristol BS16 9JB
(this address not for correspondence)

www.shearsman.com

ISBN 978-1-84861-847-3

CONTENTS

for my sisters:

Sarah born in Johor Bahru
Dorcas born in Stroud
Fiona born in Accra
Rebecca born in Derby

Whodunnit

"We are all guilty," said Doctor Williams,
head of the household, on the day he died.
The Major slept noisily in an armchair.
The lid of his glass eye was flicked back.
He could have been a winking corpse.
Open on his lap was an Agatha Christie,
Murder on the Orient Express.
Stanley, the ex-wrestler, exercised
a yo-yo. It described greater and greater
ellipses, the orbits of the planets.
By the sundial Miss Elsie Sutcliffe
dictated the first clue, "To my loyal subjects."

In the blue room Lady Amanda had woken.
She rehearsed the customary questions.
"Am I clay or root? Am I stem or leaf,
bud or flower? What did my dream mean;
the church with the diamond-shaped west window,
myself in mourning and my hands so wrinkled?"
She noticed the seams at the room's corners
widening until a slow avalanche of earth
slid rumbling slightly until it settled.
She watched lichen and moss accumulate.
A fern sprouted from her shoulder
its tip curled like a baby's fist.

1974

A Haunting

Something is crawling up the side of the house.
It has been all my life.
Bony or scaly, it's not ivy or clematis,
but a matter of belief.

Someone not entirely friendly is dancing on the roof
though his rhythm can't be caught.
Neither waltz nor jig nor galloping hoof
that tapping could be fate.

Breath that's icy cold spirals up from the cellar
and speaks with a serpent's hiss.
The fire that enchanted like a storyteller
dies away to wordlessness.

It's not the cat on the doorstep, the dog whining
for me to let him in.
It's not a bird or the wind in the chimney,
but my sense of mortal sin.

For this is not how I thought love would call to me.
It chills me like winter rain.
Neither angelic nor human nor beastly
it whispers to me in pain.

Siberian Irises

All day there's been the tremulous
impersonal rattle of a whitethroat's song
as it delves for insects in the valleys
and ridges of the apricot's bark.

A wasp with a red abdomen sneers
over the winter garden's glass roof
above which a ghost of gold and sky-blue
shimmers behind gauzy net curtains.

And so our vision hesitates down
to the irises whose indigo
has a recollection of red
and something of the dark between the stars.

In forty-eight hours they've altered
from black dogmatic spearheads to the curve
and countercurve of petals round a tongue,
pistils feathered with stamens, mild milky white.

Tomorrow they'll have withered to twists
of ancient carbon paper, all while the moon
moves from incompletion through perfect form
to a Roman coin clipped on one side,

all while you change from apparition
at an upstairs window through flesh and blood
to shrivelling scorn as the whitethroat sings
my fortune like dice clattering in a cup.

Thaw

Our world today is melting.
The red arcs of the creeper
bend and shake with beaded light
continually sliding
to the point where a twig ends
its own non-Euclidean form,
so water drops on to mulch
which stirs under the impact.

Now your hair is much thicker.
You've washed, dried and twisted it
into a braid whose gold sparks
with light when you comb it out
and my gaze is held there by
electromagnetic force.

Weeding

Once more I grub up ground elder from the soil
corpse-white rhizomes fashioning networks as I labour,
one fibre stretching itself the entire
interior groove in a concrete tile
I'd split and used in the grass's border.

I trowel and sift inch by inch until I dislodge
a walnut shell filled with clay and the larvae
of ants glittering with rage like tiny bronze nails.
They run all over my hand, pinprick and blotch
my skin with formic acid molecules.

Zero tolerance for our garden's terrorists.
You see the walnut shell and claim I've destroyed
a universe. You're far too kind to all things green.
for you ground elder is as worthy as a rose.
You can't bear to pull up the useless and the plain.

So let green flourish. Thirty years ago I had a bedroom
in shades of green. One evening, the rest
of the shared house being busy, I invited
a Russian pupil there whose English I had to test
for a Master's course. She hesitated.

On entering she said the colours reminded her
of interrogation in the Lubyanka.
We laboured inch by inch through her text above
a noisy dinner party, changing round 'a' and 'the'.
Afterwards we thought better of making love.

A Cellar Room on to a Garden

i.m. Teodor Babin (1930–1995)

It faces west so the light is always soothing,
a room like childhood, but not my own
with items from a village near the Polish border
and a flat near the railway track to Hungary;
this year's red wine fermenting in a demijohn,
a bubble rising in the glass valve every second,
a yellow pumpkin, football-sized, and pumpkin seeds,
which taste like spearmint, a dripping tap.

Two woodcuts – an ash tree in late autumn
and a road to the little town of Somewhere
with its church, council hall and granary –
orange heads of flowers, which will be cooked
into an ointment for every human ill,
seven bottles of blackcurrant syrup,
a legendary divan from the kitchen of the flat
near the railway track, a doll with a skirt
made by my daughter, a box of glass balls
for a Christmas tree, a creamer, sunglasses,
a jar of apricot preserves, a dripping tap.

A wind-up clock with a face in imitation
mother-of-pearl and brass hands stuck at ten-to-four,
a philodendron in a pot on a crystal cake stand
trailing over a nineteen fifties radio,
make Opera, finished in walnut veneer –
I look at the dial of frequencies: Sackville, Praha,
Schwarzenberg, Tel Aviv, Nice, Stalingrad,
Hilversum, Moorside Edge, Athlone – a dripping tap.

The window is shaded by dark red flowers,
the garden a lawn, two conifers, vegetables
which feed us and fruit trees; peach, apricot,

cherry, plum and an underground store for potatoes,
finally the fence, outside which my father-in-law
once sat and said to me – I will translate –
"During the war we had to learn German at school,
after the war Russian. I will not learn English,"
and he stared across the fields and houses to the west
as if he thought he'd see clouds of dust again
from armoured vehicles and soldiers marching.

Old Bolshevik Poet with Nuthatch

Yesterday the apricots showed pinkish points
from gnarled minute dragon claws.
Today I struggle to recall
the peculiar rosy haze they cast
across the garden and the past.

The pear still has buds sticky to the touch.
The apple trees extend glints of green
towards a qualitative change and shape.
White apricot blossom under the sun
explodes and revolution has begun.

Are you with us or against us? I ask
a busy comrade with blue-grey wings
and light mustard-coloured breast scuttling
downwards to probe the bark of an apple tree.
He pauses and looks askance at me.

A loud call, a flutter to a second tree.
He strops his beak before a trilling scold.
Are you with us or against us? I ask.
A hard official stare is his reply
through the Zorro mask around his eyes.

I have retired and let history move on,
my freckles replaced by liver spots,
my joints aching as the clouds come down.
A cold flurry hints that winter could return
from an east where farms and villages burn.

Apricot Brandy

The only gold we had was from the barrel
in the off-licence managed by a Pole.

Cheaper than sherry, it poured slower than oil.
Customers had to bring their own bottle

otherwise the Pole frowned and said "No dice."
I'd bring a decanter of cut glass.

Over a fortnight we'd see the colour sink
to emptiness, leaving only a chink

the afterglow of the sun when it has slipped
over the horizon. Our tumblers tipped

for the last drop. "Lang may your lum reek!"
we'd murmur and we wouldn't ever speak

of what had wounded us, our father's absence.
I'd never tasted a flavour so intense.

Since then other apricots, marhulovica,
baratskovica or kajsijovaca,

have neither drop nor scent nor colour of my past
even when drunk slowly and made to last.

I can sip and savour them all from the roof
of my mouth to my throat. At fifty percent proof

they numb my tongue, make nonsense of my speech
and the bittersweetness I still try to reach.

Alchemy

The signs were there for all to see.
Red ants raised little dirt volcanoes
from cracks in the gazebo's masonry.

Fruit dropped from creaking trees on cue
each windfall more circular than the last
and colouring to a blush's hue.

Our manuscripts were carelessly left out.
Their ink ran like witch's blood and scorched the grass
so nothing healthy would ever sprout.

The laurel was transformed by ill will.
Wind could not stir leaves which yet moved
when the air was absolutely still

as though they were lips round dark mouths
babbling above mould and loam where neither
bird hopped nor lizard scuttled. Truths

beyond our hearing's pitch were uttered.
We slowed the noise down octaves, reversed it.
All we heard was meaningless mutter.

Having the Boys Over

Who will tumble from the sky
and be arrested in my garden
disentangling themselves from a parachute?

Who will thrust up through the soil
and brush crumbs from their heads and shoulders
staring goggle-eyed waist deep in our cabbage patch?

And who will flit like a bat
intent on catching moths and midges
claiming they are between heaven and the earth?

None of my friends, I suspect,
though of those who are outrageous
some still love their wives, some still believe in God.

We look up at shooting stars.
The ground beneath our feet is unmoved.
Something dark in the air shies by very fast.

Humming-Bird Hawk-Moth

I saw you a month ago
among the final clusters of honey-suckle
and now by our window box,
wingwhirr a brown and yellow mist in miniature
above your pointed body
whose antennae are waxed handlebar moustaches
rolled to a wiry thinness,
whose abdomen terminates in a mottled wedge
like the tail feathers of a hawk.

The handbook tells me you migrate in spring
and that the eggs you lay singly
in Lady's Bedstraw won't survive our sharp winter.
Yet here you are, hornet-sized,
tongue as long as your body kinking in the middle
while you dip into the red mouths
of our Bizzie Lizzies at the end of this long summer.

A Garden Spider

I'm still much too afraid to want to try
and place you in the palm of my hand
which the span of your legs would almost straddle
even though I'm too thick-skinned for your venom.

I can make out the pinpoint oil drop glint
of your eight eyes as you shift furtively
to the shelter of a gap between
a border of half bricks and the wall

withdrawing behind lupins and roses
and the sinister Virginia creeper
that smothers what it overgrows leaving all
bereft of light while you just devour woodlice.

You aren't disgusting. Your jointed brown legs
are like wood splints, camouflage against birds.
You scuttle from me like an academic
who detests teaching, who hides in her research.

At the end of the garden your spindlier
lighter-coloured cousins have spread their silk
on top of our hedge to catch mosquitoes.
They ripple and shimmer in the fitful air

until the webs become crests of a wave
about to topple on three conifers
that we planted, the dark turquoise masts and shrouds
of a ship submerged in the summer earth.

September

An apricot left unpicked in August
has wrinkled on its twig so that its skin,
coloured like a sun squinted at through dust,
possesses the folds and contours of a brain.

A Camberwell Beauty, old, to judge by wings
with frayed yellowing edges like worn silk, floats
down every ten minutes and unrolls a tongue,
curved like a long black eyelash, to the apricot,

which must be fermenting as the insect's flight
becomes unsteadier and unsteadier.
It is the soul of a Chinese poet
whose verse and life were always much too sober,

unwilling to enter that space, which is neither
this life nor the next, after many glasses
of chrysanthemum wine. Now desire
compels it to suck at a sweet lack of neatness

until a disorder in the air shakes the tree
and all the poets rise; Camberwell, Peacock,
Red Admiral, towards an assembly
of birds whose songs and appetites now unlock.

Sickle Moon

The orchard shadows are mottled and where I step they are slightly damp from the rain which drips from the eaves of the shed through a complex of angles of leaning timber on to the top of a steel drum.

A Great Tit finishes feeding from the bark of the branch of an apple tree with a complacent "chink, chink," as though it had fed at a rather good restaurant. It removes itself to another branch where it is rather difficult to make out against the colour of the leaves, the twigs and the blue sky behind, although ten minutes of slight movement in the leaves from it preening grit or parasites or the last fledgling down make me fairly certain of its position.

The young bird roosts above the raspberry canes. Its round breast emulates the roundness of unripe apples and its black head blends in with the leaves.
It knows less than me, but not much less.

A sickle moon has risen before the sun has set, a white curve like the scar on the thigh of a girl I met in a disco club.

Later I followed the shape of the scar with my fingertips. Its texture was smooth and cold as silver. She didn't answer when I asked how she came by such a wound.

"Look at the old man in the moon," she said, "And his wicked smile."

Nightowl

Closing my eyes, I float
above wooded coastline,
my bones filled with air, appetite
ravenous for the least detail
which might creep from shelter.
Opening them I start to move,
not sleep-walking, but not grounded
in the yellow distance to bed
or glass minute of undressing.

I seem to move near waves
which scrape shingle with a sound
like thick curtains tugged together.
Each step I take ruffles plush.
You're not bleached by moonlight
but planished. You turn to me
shoulders sleek as ivory
and your gestures reach
to abundances of maize.

Then you return my beliefs,
that we'll be too careful,
that each cry won't fledge
fully to the owl's quivering
single-minded vowel.
"Why hover?" you say.
Stooping over you I hear
the sea's neutral ease. Gliding
my hands touch, hook round your hips.

1976

Autumn Coming On

Someone is running very fast
to catch you up and breathe down your neck.
The clouds have lifted at last.
Not that they have anything to do
with your pursuer's ultimate intentions,
but they just have to show
that that pitter patter behind you
remains however much the weather changes.

What is it that you've done
to make someone so determined?
All summer long the sun shone down
on the fruit you picked, the wasps that worried.
What possessed you to say aloud a truth
so irrelevant and cruel?
That rustling at your back is not the scurry
of falling leaves, but what you cannot face.

Someone whose love you may have lost
is walking steadily ahead.
The vapours you breathe out may turn to frost
before they touch her even though
her stride is leisurely as if she wanted you
to fall in step beside her.
You lag behind as your neck begins to glow
from breath too hot for summer, too cold for winter.

The End of the Affair

So the cat untwists in midair
beneath the apple tree, a blackbird
fluttering backwards from her paws
as she lands eyes vivid with desire,
crouches, wriggles, deliberates, blinks.
So, too, an apple springs unbitten
from your hand to its twig, unripens
from red to green, dwindles to pistil,
before it blossoms, folds into bud.

So, too, the car strikes, tyres then brakes screech,
your father's walking stick flying
to his grasp as he somersaults
to his feet, backs off to his house,
goes inside, floats his coat to a hook, sits
over the years his hair thickening,
darkening, his voice deepening
into laughter until he can catch
and throw you up to where you smile.

So, too, the scar on your thigh,
whose slight ridge I love to touch
with a fingertip, widens
becoming bluish, livid, pink,
minute particles rising to it
from wherever you care to limp
making a scab, an ooze of droplets,
a flow before another's knife
withdraws and heals the jagged tear.

So, too, our lips close on each other's.
So, too, our mouths move apart.
So, too, their separate smiles fade.
So, too, our eyes look askance.

So, too, we step back, turn away.
So, too, our heartbeats decelerate.
So, too, we don't blurt out the words.
So, too, we don't decide to risk it.
So, too, we are never introduced.

Quince Tree

There's a quince tree with fruit across the street
below me in a neighbour's garden.
I recall a black-and-white illustration
of such a tree, just after I'd learned to read,
in a book of fairy tales or saints' stories
with suffering about to happen and last
until a happy ending or salvation.

I look at the quince tree and its hard fruit,
round and yellow against the dark green leaves.
Beyond are brown-leafed chestnuts, the silver limbs
of a birch, many-armed Shiva dancing
in front of a rectangular office block
over which is the pale blue evening sky
without a trace of cloud, infinite, empty.

Pies and Toads

First there were sausage pies in Aberdeen,
the edges of the pie crusts Presbyterian
without adornment, perfect flaking circles.

I ate them at Great-Uncle Alexander's,
kept back from enlistment as the youngest brother,
the one without the gift of the gab

who, asked to break bad news of a death
on the railways tactfully without undue pain,
said "Mother, you'll not be seeing Father again."

After pies there was a visit to the garden
to see the toad, huge, motionless and sullen,
but not from a diet of sausage pie.

I was prompted to be as courageous
as Great-Uncle Willie killed at Arras
and kneel down and with both hands pick up the toad

moving Great-Uncle Alec to eloquence;
"Your Auntie Bella has often said
that there's a jewel in the centre of its head."

I learnt to make pies myself under the care
and protection of the state when my father
had neglected to pay a number of school bills.

The home used to be a hunting lodge of King Charles.
I was treated like royalty, hidden from girls
and boys, who'd become no longer girls or boys,

in a kitchen where I rubbed flour and fat
into lumps as large as toads, rolled them out
for a filling of onion and corned beef.

The cook told me that I had the temperament,
an eye for detail and the right equipment,
the dry, cold hands of a pastry chef or hangman.

The Abandoned Garden

Do we leave the abandoned garden
by the river where ducks perch on stones,
fish point their whiskery snouts upstream
and the current sibilates on sand
and gravel as if it were something
of consequence to be repeated?
Do we leave the abandoned garden
to the politics of the bypass
on the other side where traffic bawls
interrupted by ambulances?

There's not much to put the eye at ease
when we pass the abandoned garden;
tangles of string, planks and chicken wire,
a smother of snowdrops in late spring,
a quince tree with lichen, yellow fruit
rotting to brown then a winter black.
Is there a forgotten expression
in the language for which the bleak phrase
'abandoned garden' is not enough?
They'll build a gas station in its place.

Yet it's almost better to linger
and gaze at the abandoned garden
than move on a hundred yards or so
to the road bridge across the river
and bronze statue with blurred inscription
dedicated to Saint Someone-Else,
erected under a sycamore
by families who emigrated,
where now boys without gardens gather
to share cigarettes and deal hard drugs.

Tea and Poetry

This was the England he'd always feared
would come about through his inattention,
a woman with an ample bosom
reading a poem about a hairy ape
holding a candelabra above her head
as they mount the stairs to a large cage
while her husband tends his tomato plants.

He himself sits nibbling a buttered scone
quite unable to subdue a tumescence
which has troubled him on and off since morning.
Shouldn't the woman with the bosom
understand and let him take her panties down?
Her husband returns with digital shots
of beef toms. The ape is nowhere to be found.

On the radio an opera begins
dissonant yet tuneful enough to provide
a talking point for at least ten minutes.
Its music spreads like the musky scent
of wet bracken over a landscape
of stone walls, sheep pens and cottages
where parents saw their children in half.

A Municipal Fountain in Autumn

Between the trucks bound for Turkey gasping
out of the main road's bend as their brakes release
and the slipshod eddies of the river
where red finned barbel shimmy against the current
a concrete fountain sporadically sprays
its water among birch, willow, blue fir and yew.

Close up its base looks like a boletus mushroom
though the water patters in a basin
whose design imitates the neo-classical
ambitions of a down-at-heel Hapsburg town.
A crack zigzags from the ground to the basin's lip
and "Tatran 98" has been daubed there in green paint.

Neither celestial nor iniquitous
it is a place where teenage girls meet to smoke,
boys to pop the tabs on cans of beer,
derelicts to sit on the fountain basin's edge
and pass a plastic bottle from hand to hand
as the fountain soars, sputters, dribbles, runs dry.

On the nearby benches old men and women
with faces like beige counterpanes where shapes have slept
leaving creases which can't be straightened out
go over who might have been correct years ago,
a muttering the fountain's splashing echoes,
a wasting, wasted, waste speech carried off by drains

while dogs and owners, neither young nor old, stroll by
and the fountain unaccountably stops
then starts as they cross the road to where leaves
have floated down in avenues between houses
from lime trees pollarded so often the twigs stick up
punkish from knobbly heads on twisted torsos.

From my attic window I can see the fountain
its basin almost shining as the night comes down.
I cross the room to watch verticals of white smoke
from the rows of houses stretching westwards
towards the hills as if a school of dragons
had landed and were at rest breathing easily.

Out Walking After Rain

White trumpets of flowers lean
from the bindweed that plaits
a fence of chicken wire
behind which three plastic buckets,
blue, pink and yellow, lie
beside an armchair left out
so long its legs are wormholed,
its green upholstery rotted,
and a table whose top has warped
leaving a concavity
where rain has laid a mirror
so clear I could gaze into it
and forget my origins.

Beyond the table and the chair
a dozen Canada geese
graze until they see I'm there
and then they lift their thick necks
and orange bills with a stare
sidelong and glazed as porcelain
while I'm distracted by the glare
of a cyclist shoving a bike
whose tyres are bereft of air.

Pronouns

for John Welch

What would the rest of us make of the pronouns without you?

Their transparent forms might all at once become opaque.

They'd be motes and beams in the eyes of their beholders,
smoke and cloud moulding as a solid architecture,
towers, basilicas, the word as force, as dogma.

Speech would be blown about like a kite in a high wind
as the proper names try to take down their umbrellas.

Griefs would bend into the gale homewards to permanence.

The pronouns would encumber our lives more than ever.

That 'I' would take up a bedroom wall,
a wardrobe nobody will take off our hands.

With you around, the pronouns are light as airborne seed
taking root and blooming in and out of lives.

They multiply in sentences until clipped back
to their appropriate place in the infinite sentence language is supposed to be
though lives are not sentences where we serve time
until released into some sort of bliss of repetition:
the language of paradise row on row of tonsured pronouns
chanting "pro nobis, pro nobis."

Lives are sayings leafy with names which incline towards any source of light
then stop mid-sentence before we think we are quite done.

Say on, I say, say …

Elegy

for John Hartley Williams (1942–2014)

What would you make of the four drunkards
with their cans of beer and plastic bottles
of plum brandy, home-distilled, 50% proof,

grouped round a stone cross dedicated
to Saint Obscure the Barfly beside a river
rain has turned from a sidle into a rout

and engaged in earnest conversation
like a sideshow in a School of Athens canvas
painted by a minor baroque master,

one stressing with excessive emphasis
the wrong syllables in complex words,
the second listening as though he might

disapprove of Socrates, the third stuttering
objections and the fourth staring away
his mouth gaping as if the void possessed him?

Possibly nothing, John, though you're no longer here
to spare them a glance, scoff or grin in assent.
You might point out that the philosophers

seem to be speaking in a language
entirely new to the human race
though it might just be the river growling

fifty yards away from where they discourse.
Perhaps I should join in and tell them
that a friend I never met face-to-face is gone

and that they should look at the river
to see how dangerous the floating world can be,
that tumbling willow stump, that doll without a head.

They might offer me a long hard pull
from the darkest-tinted plastic bottle
and then I'd speak in unknown tongues, too,

before stumbling back home for an early sleep
waking later to gaze at the speechless stars
as they recede from me very fast.

Anxiety

On the hillside a tractor and cart
take advantage of a break in the weather.

I'm going home to feed the dog
and eat a ladle or two of goulash.

The swollen river is flecked like café au lait,
otherwise a jostle of twigs and plastic bottles.

One more storm and it'll rise another yard
and the water table will seep up into my cellar.

I pass a drunk going through his possessions
unsteadily laying them out on a bench.

What has he lost? What has he lost?
and I walk onwards to a row of poplar stumps

among them a second bench on which
a heavily pregnant girl talks hopefully

to a boy with yellowish dreadlocks
who leans away from her staring across the river.

The dog is anxious when I get home
circling me, his nails clicking on the parquets,

squatting on the bag I leave in the hall
then barking when I leave so I can hear him

all the way down the street to the path
where I walk again beside the swollen river.

The couple have gone back to where they came from
to be replaced by a neater girl and boy

in sensible cardigans holding hands.
The drunk is taking his things out again

from his hold-all for the umpteenth time.
What has he lost? What has he lost?

The tractor and cart have reached the crest of the hill.
The river froths, bubbles and hisses onwards.

I have forgotten to check my cellar.

Snow

The ultimate poem on snow
should stop twittering right now
as the noise drains from the town
and the cars and lorries slow.
All you can hear is the light
at the pedestrian crossing
clicking too loud to be the slight
alarms of a redstart fussing
that you're dangerous or too soft
on the magpie harassing
blue tits away from your gift
of bacon, leaving them bereft.

The ultimate poem on snow
should stop as traffic clears its throat
to swish and grunt through a show
of entropy although
the snowfall outlines poplar,
cherry, fir and ash bough by bough
as if it could denature
colour from the trees until they're
two-dimensional, an unsure
grey, black and white like a graveyard
where nothing moves anymore
so you glance upwards to stare

at gravity's remorseless
tug on the almost weightless
fragmented flakes whose feckless
eddying to and fro
confuses and you can't know
if what you see is almost dance
or almost not dance
as you follow the footprints

in the ultimate poem on snow
blurred by the continuance
of white on white whose radiance
pricks when the wind begins to blow.

Winter Music

Outside cold drags us down to minus ten degrees.
I've yet to shake the snow from our conifers
beyond which the streets run parallel to one another
their vanishing point under steep hills once patched
with orchards never lit by the orange street lamps.

No-one walks out, though on the radio a dance
from heat quickens on a guitar to abandon,
sounding where snow falls rarely on the glossy leaves
of orange trees growing in long parallels
and even then it turns to vapour upon the grass.

The guitarist's fingers could be at minus ten degrees,
their touch exact and gentle as the falling snow
on strings not quite parallel to one another
where the notes walk out like folk acquainted
with one another shading their eyes against the light.

Nursery Rhymes

i.m. Allen Tate (1899–1979)
"most verse is written accidentally"

ABC
the bouncing bee
the cat's in the cupboard
and can't see me

though I'd like to see
one of your whiskery greycoat ghosts
lead out heroic shades for me,

firstly, of my father
who drove a burning tank in Italy
away from his camp to safety,

secondly, of my grandfather
in 1919, almost free
after sixteen failed escape attempts,

engaged in a market gardening course
in a Dutch transit camp
somewhere near the Zuider Zee

which is to say DEF
ghosts muttering or screeching
songs for the deaf
pitched far too high
even for the hearing of a dog

or way beneath the bass clef
and jungle rumble of the elephant
wishing not to be eavesdropped
except by its own kind
who have no alphabet

and thereby
can't deny
the truth of GHI
and pie in the sky
where all the seas gang dry
of what flows down from the Rock Candy mountains

and where there is no vision
to drink up or down
except that blasted eye
in the sky
with an iris flecked with thunderclouds
and a black sun in the centre

whose black light creates no shadow
for adherents of last things and JKL,
an acronym of the Fall
long past with my father
when to pose with a cigarette,
Senior Service as I recall,
conveyed something of style
not from despair, but from knowing
that knowing nothing except
we have just the one A to Zed or Zee
attracts a stellar quality
like shades to blood sacrifice:

Ginger, Fred, Carole, Clark, Mae and Cary,
their style a steal, no, that stole
the rump and tail of something silvery
which she wore once at a funeral
at whose wake I drank too much
and played the fool
until she took me home,
instead of telling me
to go to hell,
and caused me to find myself,

well before the middle of my life
in a flat in Saint Leonard's-on-Sea,
instructed in the sexual
and not completely impossible.

I met her again thirty-six years on
in the New Tate by a prospect of London
at its most august, sand-blasted neoclassical.
Fish now spawn anew in the turbid flow between.

Just so
MNO
cabbage, carrot, parsnip and potato,
grandfather's precise but kindly accent,

lettuce in the summer,
onions grenade-hard,

skins the colour of a bruise,
to look at them made our eyes water.

Memory is so physical,
the future just mystical.

At present I'd like to know
what art has left to show,

contrariwise if there can be power
in restraint and concealment any more.

Impossible to return carrots or beef
back through Granny's wrought iron grinder

and then to a fine upstanding vegetable
with its filigree spray of leaf

or to a prime cut, then carcase
of the bullock tap-dancing on the roof

whose mother jumped over the moon
into a pickled quandary of recollection

of Ps and Qs I've minded
just to stop the Rs unwinding

my sense of decorum
as I exercise a North British skill

and rock 'n' roll 'em
to an unEnglish extreme

rrround that rrrugged rrrock
wherrre the rrragged rrrascal rrran,

a sour-faced man fingering his wounds
and uttering vague piteous sounds

becoming after school was over
a rustling in boxtree and yew,

Simple Stu who'd emerge and write
his name in the earth with a stick.

STU,
the book of rhymes was baby blue,
large type and pictures,
Little Jack Horner looking smug,
Little Bo Peep without a clue.

It was the first thing I read
in the big brick house on top of the hill.
Fifty years on I found a copy in a library sale
just after I'd learnt a lifetime friend was dead.

And all Father Time said was hickory dickory dock
back in that house where I read my first book.

No hearse ever passed our gate, just the Corona truck;
Limey-lemons, cherryades, dandelion and burdocks.

VWX
not a flavour of a soda pop,
but a core group of letters
on a British number plate
circa the late nineteen-fifties.

Having then moved on from poetry to fiction,
I'd award myself chapters of *Doctor Dolittle*
to be read before I turned off the light,
according to the number of three-letter words
I'd spot on Sunday excursions in the Vanguard
through picturesque nursery garden England.

Fox, cox, axe, tax, hex, six, fix
and the Latin I'd begun;
dux, lux, nux, light eternal, a nut,
or the inconsequential. I have not
forgotten the Latin number sex,
but never saw that on a number plate.

Sufficient chapters awarded I'd drift away
to somewhere between thought and childish rhyme.
In the opposite lane the cars hummed by;
bix, bax, box, bux, buxom, buxum,
the branches of boxwood, a poet's flute.
The smell of petrol and its husky softness a paradox.

Once, the Vanguard crammed with his children, my regrettable
and lost, regretted father passed a burning fiery furnace
from which flecks of paper or something even more fragile
floated up like flocks of small red birds that sang and turned to ash.

YZ
Go to bed!
my father said.
Time for bed, from Grandpa
as he stroked my head.

Wee Willie Winkie
still runs through the town
dowsing each gas light
as the dark comes down.
And more on my street
has he snuffed out
than stay burning this short night.

Folk Songs

The songs have little to do with clouds
although clouds change shape and lurch
like old women in layers of black skirts
on Sundays clutching their prayer books to church.

Nobody is cloud-struck or looks beyond their nose.
Their gaze is earthwards and they sing, shadowed
by years of hunger, drought and flood,
joy never easy, always to be winnowed,

Johnny home from the wars and coughing blood,
black-eyed girls sulky with discontent,
swallows squealing their signals from elsewhere
as the clouds dawdle and fragment.

Green

Greenness has come thickly to the eye;
the apple blossom's pink and white
almost completely blown away,
magnolia having shed what could be
shiny purple shells of lizard eggs.

Lime pollen scratches at my throat.
Black junipers creep up the hills
like conspirators in cloaks.
Just to feel what it was I used to hope
once more sensation by sensation!

It won't happen. No girl will emerge
from underneath the chestnut tree,
the light turning raindrops to pearls
on a face upturned and demure
yet saying "Risk everything!"

Clouds disperse, mountains briefly show
lion shapes as the dark replaces green.
I'll renew as best as I know how
watching while stars rise then slip down,
my hands splayed, two leaves lacking green.

From Stillness

i.m. Christopher Middleton (1926–2015)

i
The liquid geometry of the clouds,
wave forms, helices of thermals,
grey and white shapes under blue absence of form.
suggest cause, suggest effect
though it's foolish to try and join one to the other,
as if even weather were an argument
while the clouds twist, come apart and vanish,
and madness to believe that vision
proceeds from me in a straight line
crossing the universe all the way back.

ii
A pair of chiff-chaffs,
blown back and forth by the wind,
perched on the top twigs
of my older apricot,
ride out random gusts
flying free when they desire.
Each wing beat lifts them
slightly so they rise and glide
a shallow wave form
as though mimicking sea-swell.

iii
The five-petalled star of dog rose
sheds itself quickly
to manufacture an itch of sweetness,
a pentagon of scent
containing the hexagons of sugars;
pentagram, hexagram,
a grimoire or the *I Ching*,
the will to power, the will to stillness.

What has this to do with my wife's sixth sense,
my daughter's sixth toe removed soon after birth?

iv
A field of blue vetch and white poppies
with a single apple tree
under which my daughter rests
legs crossed in the lotus position
while her daughter runs round and round
the tree whose trunk spirals clockwise
after years of obedience to the sun
whose heat has dispersed the clouds.
All the trees in the nearby forest
grow straight, competing for the light.

Winter Express at Dawn

We've been swallowed up and now gaze
from within the beast halfway along
a glowing spine in a demon's body
whose brutal bellow leaps ahead of us
between banks of snow as its head beam
sweeps across hill crests like a huge firefly
until the express slows between sepulchres
of factories and tenements
lit with votive lamps for those about
to resurrect into a red dawn
where magenta, vermilion, orange
become briefly flames, ember spark,
less a rebirth more an intention,
a thought about rebirth, a thought
about a thought, daybreak, distance.

Rosa Canina

On a Sunday afternoon waiting for a train
red poppies like sudden children's laughter,
miniature pyramids of purple vetch
between the sleepers in a disused siding,
elderberry spreading irregular shapes
of genteel lace handkerchiefs in spotless white,
a bush of pink dog rose into whose fragile cups
I and the insect population dip for a scent
impermanent as the lovely wisp of a girl
between boyfriends I once spent the night talking to,
afterwards she refusing my invites to dinner,
to the cinema, even for another drink,
then vanishing from the university,
diploma work unwritten, exams untaken,
to be met later by chance on a mountain
hefting ropes and crampons, coming down
as I was going up, pausing for ten minutes
before vanishing again until one night
a ring on my doorbell and there she was
(she never said how she got hold of my address)
still a lovely wisp with a thick braid of brown hair
unravelling down her naked back as she recalled
our first conversation and what I failed
to perceive or say or do, gone before I woke
the words on the note she left like seeds from rose hips
dropped down the back of my shirt for a joke
leaving an itch for someone as brief as dog rose,
thornier, tougher than I ever could suppose.

Entering Hungary

i. from Slovakia

On my way again at dawn
under wedges of cloud
from which a broken alphabet
of crows tumbles above ripe maize,
lines of osier along the brooks,
a lone pear tree in a meadow
no-one has cultivated,
gravel pits, windbreaks
of poplar, sunflowers,
houses with shutters up,
a ploughed field of maroon earth,
bulbs of water tanks on columns
like giant stalks of garlic.
My cell phone chimes,
a new network claiming
I'm entering Hungary,
then a copper beech, silver birch
in a railway station garden
beside which a blue train starts up,
rain streaming from its windows,
on a branch line curving off
to somewhere under the last hill
before the plains of Pannonia
and villages with wickerwork
dressed with bouquets to honour
their lovely unwed daughters.

ii. from Serbia

After the reedy ditches and black earth
for papery yellow stalks of maize,
a field with a flock of grazing geese,
then the rusty chassis of a truck
before a scrub of hazel up to
loops of razor wire on the border.
At Kelebia a guard taps the wheels
of our train, cigarette in one hand
a long metal hammer in the other.
There's honeysuckle growing on the side
of an office beside the platform
next to a linden on which a push-bike leans
that the guard mounts as we pull away.

iii. from Romania

An old yellow dog
with a grey muzzle
crosses the railway tracks,
a limping but happy dog
with a black collar.
He sniffs around the base
of a garbage can
casts a sidelong glance at me,
takes note and hobbles on.

Quince trees by the shed
for the customs men
have blossomed reddish pink
the colour of a blouse
of a girl called Cynthia
would wear at grammar school.
She'd tease me every day
and refused to dance with me,
"Not you, not you, not you."

Thunder clouds have thickened.
So it'll rain on the limping
contented yellow dog
who's lifted a leg beside
the Cynthia-coloured quince
and now checks under goods trucks
until his owner,
who's just stamped my ticket,
whistles him aboard.

Ring doves on the gable ends
of the station master's office
gurgle and coo themselves hoarse.
Romanian from students
next to me and scuffling
as the limping dog climbs
the metal steps, enters
our compartment, sniffs, leaves
going about his business.

On the Polish Border

The wind's fitful this evening
lifting the long strands
of ivy drooping from the roof
to reveal a plastic tray.

Friable pieces have snapped off
round a pattern of daisies
with mustard-coloured centres
and solar flares of petals.

There's a sister tray of poppies
on the dresser inside
beneath blue mottoes hand-stitched
on clean cotton tacked to the wall.

We kiss and tease each other
into the goose feather quilt
with rumours of brown bears seen
ambling in the upper field.

We did watch short-tailed deer
graze on the hill, a wild pig
break cover from the forest,
a marten shimmying through grass

and a slope of cherry blossoms
like a shout in the silence
of the dense green pine and beech
through which wind suddenly hurtled

sweeping their whiteness downwards
until they sprang back as if shocked,
a gust not to be repeated
anywhere else at any time.

On the Kosovo Border 2008

Jagged the fell tops, the light failing,
soldiers filing to Ground Safety Zone.
The tanks are kept in working order
though none hope they'll be employed again.
One creaks on to its transporter tracks
like an old man, overweight and in pain.

Downstairs the well-briefed conscript boy
simpers, "It was ever thus," unable
to utter anything less schoolmasterly
and shepherds us to his stiff-necked pal,
the major who once penned a monograph
on the seven chapels up on the hill.

Spick and span the barrack courtyard
with not a cigarette butt in sight.
The pines were planned at an equal space
from one another and through them, slight
and pale the commander comes to greet us,
severe, but a man none has cause to hate.

Yellow as the sere leaves the liquor served
in regulation glasses, bitter the pleasure
sipped slowly as our reports are heard.
Agreed and minuted the measures
we request, then dinner, relaxation
with a trove of battalion treasures.

Unlit our departure down the narrow lanes,
cloudy the night, no starshine lifts our gaze,
only seven havering lamps upon the hill
where boar and badger trot down ways
unreasoning fanatics might follow
bearing grudges, bringing violent days.

Vision

It is near winter in Celestial County,
flat clouds over mountains ribbed with early snow,
meadows cropped by sheep to a fuzz of brown roots,
the river still flowing, a moving mirror.

I have scrambled up through beech and tall pine
from my cabin to a sparser fantasy,
an avenue of aspen, clusters of birch
behind which could be shapes of beasts I can't name.

I wish to see the angels who ride up here
on their grey stallions, high in the saddle
yet easy at a gallop, Wyoming style,
their yelps neither anathema nor blessing.

But the space is empty, the distances meek.
Above me I watch a hawk fold its wings and drop.

In the Mountains

Everything's larger in the mountains.
Butterflies have broader wings
for flight in the rarefied air.
There are rowan, birch and pine from which
cones hang like wooden purses.

The namesake of a war criminal
has been chopping wood for three days
hefting an orange-handled axe.
Behind him three hunting dogs bark
at the nonchalant passage of a cat.

The gardens are untended.
Sow thistle, harebell, burdock sprout
among spinach and peonies
whose white blooms, the fists of infants
tightly clenched, have yet to open.

The mountains are a pure place to be.
Girls and boys shed a tooth or two,
but not their virtue until they leave
seldom wanting to return.
Much older they talk of their birthplace,

but without nostalgia citing
quarrels with mothers or fathers
which may have never happened.
Just now it rains heavily
on the steep russet metal roofs

of houses down which the rain flows
then drops in rippling vertical strings
of glass beads. The old sit behind them
on their decks drinking coffee,
shawls round their shoulders against the cold.

The Haunted Temple

A narrative like a flight of stairs,
mottled with moss, fractured in places,
stained with the drip from the bamboo forest
either side of the naga bannisters,
likewise showing the wear and tear of years,
dragon teeth chipped, scales greasy to the touch,
is not to be relied on to instruct,
entertain or recount a simple fact.

Each stone step can be stumbled over
as a mystery or absurdity.
Two white men, brothers, approach a temple,
one hefting a parang to cut bamboo poles
and prop a grape vine for his tiny wife.
Their cautious, elderly testing of each slab,
their reluctance to touch the dragon scales
hints at lives of risks taken that sometimes failed.

Why do they wish to see such a rundown place?
Vulgar curiosity. Two monks lived there,
both healers, one so popular the other
shot him dead in a fit of jealousy.
A gecko, perched between a dragon's glare,
regards them with its orange mouth agape.
A butterfly with black wings see-saws up
and the brothers follow dourly to the top.

Should the narrative become unreliable,
without warning the steps to crack apart,
the nagas waken in a sinuous ripple
and, as the bamboo hems the brothers in,
snap at them with razor teeth while beyond
the forest, hectare after hectare
all the way to China, paragraphs of rice sprout
under drizzle which is steady, dispassionate?

Not yet and maybe never ever,
its story-telling breath as regular
as the brothers' grunting on the stairs.
The younger leans his parang against the gate
at the entrance to the temple as though he fears
demonic possession of their wits.
A young monk, five dogs and a kitten
purr, yap or grin at them in mild daylight.

Even so, will something disorderly occur?
Will they be altered in the shadows
of the temple before the gaze of Buddha,
the row of newly polished gongs, the monk's bow,
the kitten peeping round the corner,
a dog's slight snarl warning off another?
Will centuries pass before they come out
from staring at Buddha's smile and lacquered brow?

Minutes pass before different notes are struck
from the gongs and they emerge to talk in signs
with the monk whose glasses slip down his nose
when he shakes his head to show he understands
or doesn't understand that they're brothers.
They mime a quarrel and shooting with their hands
to which the monk just shrugs and responds
with another grin. Perhaps it never happened.

The brothers make their way down the dragon steps.
The black-winged butterfly rests on the scales
of a naga and permits a careful photo.
Rain still falls lightly on the bamboo and drops
splash randomly on the brothers' balding heads
as they take care not to slip. The younger
has left his parang by the gate back up the stairs.
He will be scolded with little slaps and tears.

Girls, Dogs and Depleted Uranium

The season is saucy.
Private arrangements are turned inside out
like winter gloves so that a soft,
slightly moist fur of intimacy shows upon the street.
Only the stray dogs do not canoodle.
They've been spayed or castrated,
provided with an electronic chip in their ears.
So now they lope the boulevards
uncertain of what it is they've lost
like poets for whom nothing has rung true for years.

The day is not so much pert as awry
as though a storm has been about to break
for much too long in this city
of unexplained maladies and where the talk
is of how much radiation needs to be detected
while I wait in a traffic jam
three yards from flower girls half undressed
sitting on the steps of their shop with cigarettes.
One leans forward and pants out ribbons of smoke
and I can see the wet sheen between her breasts

until I drowse away
daydreaming of stairs with bannisters curving
beneath gilded mirrors that reflect
elegant disasters, armed bands moving
across the river in spotless uniforms.
There is a fizzing volley of rifle fire,
but not loud enough for me to have to raise my voice.
I climb the stairs, your right hand on my sleeve,
a counterpoint to my unease, as your left hand lifts
the hem of the folds of snow that compose your dress.

The streets are never empty.
Even at night they're no place for a white dress
to drift as fragile as cigarette smoke
though the traffic and the heat are less.
I lose you where the stairs branch and branch again
as my eyelids rise and the flower girl dabs
with a tissue at the sweat between her breasts.
It's said the road I'm stalled upon leads to woods
where the stray dogs run seeking a coolness to stop
the bleeding from their eyes and the burning in their chests.

Pure Mathematics

Undecidable, you'll come to me, each garment
slipping off, a curved line in from the cabin door,
disordered, rumpled yet overlapping,
a novel topology of desire.

Will only the four colours of scent,
the trace of spit on the buttons of your blouse,
my touch, your throaty "Fuck me!" be sufficient
to complete the ideal map of what we'll do?

I'll tug or you'll pull, no telling whose
greater power of need will topple and fix
both of us in perfect numbers of kisses,
6, 28, 496,

as we quiver integrating the real
with the irrational square root of two
until you breathe irregularly and tremble
all along an endless random sequence

of decimal places to infinity
where your head lolls to one side and eyes close.
At sunset we'll listen to the little river tumble
while dusk gathers and multiplies its shadows.

The river will wear away its banks in bends and loops,
a ratio of pi to a crow's flight to the sea,
as an imaginary number picks her clothes up
and tenderly subtracts herself from me.

A Walk in Winter

A moral mist collects between the trees,
but it won't even start to snow.
I still can't travel from myself
for moderation dogs my heels
and the wicked give alms to beggars
while the well-behaved spank their children.

The well-behaved spoil their children.
A mortal mist thickens between the trees.
The wicked offer guns to beggars,
but they won't open fire before it snows.
Manipulation sniffs at my heels.
I still can't arm or disarm myself.

I still can't own or disown myself.
The mischievous neglect their children
while extravagance snaps at their heels
and a golden moss glows on the trees.
Like great wealth it will dazzle when it snows
and the wicked claim it's too grand for beggars.

The wicked proclaim a curse on all beggars
though I have yet to denounce myself.
My breath billows in the woods when it snows.
The misbegotten mourn the birth of children
as black frost cracks the bark of trees
and a panting negative nips their heels.

Why must the devil growl at my heels?
Who but the wicked should be beggars?
What melting mystery slips from the trees?
When is the time to resurrect myself?
How do the mad forgive their children?
Which house do we adorn when it starts to snow?

The church is lit but empty when it snows.
An innocence yaps in play at my heels.
The mild and good teach manners to their children
while the wicked blame the weather on the beggars.
I still can't believe in my soul or myself
as the mystery beckons underneath the trees.

The cold deep snow is cruel to beggars.
Only a shadow of myself whines at my heels
and there are no children underneath the trees.

Sloe Gin

for Abi and Jon

On the way down to our cabin
past the penzion that each year makes a loss
we spot a beer glass from New Year's Eve
left outside on a window sill
its beer not drunk and with a brittle head of ice.

While I struggle with bolts and locks
you walk away to gather darkness,
a scattering of sloe berries that the frost
has unembittered so you don't choke
but spit a stone out and pull a face.

Inside the cabin I discover
six hibernating peacock butterflies
stuck to the curtains, ceiling and the door jamb
folded up like pieces of burnt paper
as if they'd floated from the fireplace.

Two of them I detach from the door
fearful that I might break their wings.
I put them on a pile of history books.
They stir from reflex and show their colours,
reds, yellows, violets opening and closing.

At home we divide the sloes
between bottles, add sugar, gin, then shake.
In a week strands of violet coil upwards.
In a month the deeper shades of red will show.
We'll test the gin before the butterflies awake.

A Wasp's Nest

i.m Jon Silkin (1932–1997)

Abandoned or smoked out
it hangs from a joist in the shed
papery shreds dangling from it
around combs which are tiered
like the roof of an oriental shrine.

You were terse with acceptance,
a scrawl and "I'll take these two."
Once on a longer sequence,
"How would you like it if I sent you
a whole year's work?" Flattered, Jon.

Another wasp has tried
to pitch its tent, shaped like a yurt.
Here Tartars and Turks would raid
north-east of the ramparts
left by Aurelius's legions.

I prod the new, small white nest
with a stick. Its queen whizzes
through a gap above the joist.
"More than a little descriptive this;"
stinging, but not to destruction.

The marsh marigolds are out,
the austere Yellow Star of Bethlehem,
the pink and blue of lungwort.
Once I found "Flower Poems"
under the Roneo machine

used by "Poetry and Audience".
I sat and read them for an hour.
No-one would have marked their absence,
but I put them back next to "Preghiere"
in the editorial collection.

We met and talked just once,
in nineteen-ninety six
at a translation conference.
You were to be the victim of a hoax,
your openness to invention.

At the end I watched you leave
trundling "Stand" on a bag with wheels.
You returned my frantic wave
which I confess was actually
due to a wasp's close attention.

Small Scale Observations

i.m. Geoffrey Grigson (1905–1985)

A Pearl-bordered fritillary
wings curved like the Bugatti monoplane,
which never left the design board,
alights on moss for its morning moisture.

The buff, paper-thin lozenges,
which are the seed pods of Honesty,
two ripe microchips visible in each,
could medicate a would-be critic.

Small White, a delicacy
of muslin feeding on hawkbit
under elderberries ripening from green
to burgundy to black in umbrella clusters.

In the stream under the rocks,
miniature brown, organic tubes
from which dragonflies crawled to dry themselves
to iridescences of turquoise and cobalt.

By afternoon clouds have condensed
to billow, pop and bubble,
round and greyish like the suds which form
in a pan of boiling potatoes.

Not much later Saturn rises
lopsided with the tilt of its rings
as the clouds break up to make a backbone
with ribs sticking out from either side.

A maple leans across the point
of my territory where the stream
has descended in irregular steps
to unite with one much larger.

Tree creepers run down the maple's trunk
prodding and poking with their beaks
in the rich crevices of its bark
above scabious with rich periwigs of seed.

The fritillaries, which feed there, have dispersed
leaving a moth with tessellated
upper wings black and white, the lower scarlet,
abdomen gingery: Jersey Tiger.

At sunset my white plastic chairs
adopt the posture of skeletons
hunkered down round a darkening space
where something undefined is worshipped.

Seven brothers, he the only one
surviving war and war games;
I read his work as the Jersey Tiger
clicks its gaudy self against the lampshade.

On Looking into Clapham, Tutin and Warburg's Excursion Flora of the British Isles

The previous owner built a pool beside my cabin for a disabled child,
not much more than a bathtub and only a yard away from my deck
so the child could be safely guided down two brick steps at the near end
of the pool, which is oval in shape and thus, with the gap made by the steps,
almost in the form of the letter omega.

I've let the pool go. It's now crumbling cement and sky-blue render.
The outflow pipe has been choked by a fern and the bottom of the pool is
ridged with lines of moss. On its edges there's Herb Robert, hawsers of
bramble, saxifrage and an umbel, neither angelica nor parsley nor chervil.
So I open Clapham, Tutin and Warburg, six hundred sallow pages, as flimsy
as those in my copy of the King James Authorized Version of the Bible.

There's no need to work out if the plant is a tree, a fern or a moss and I know
an umbel when I see one. I turn to page 224, Umbelliferae, and follow the trail
to its source:

leaves not peltate, leaves variously toothed or divided,
leaves not spiny, leaves pinnate or ternate,
aerial leaves numerous and well-developed at flower,
lower leaves 2-4 pinnate or ternate,
plant glabrous: leaf margins sometimes finely toothed,
flowers white or only slightly tinged with green, pink or purple,
stems not purple spotted, bracteoles 0 or 1,
segments of lower leaves smaller, pinnatifid;
plant not rhizomatous, basal leaves soon withering;
petioles long and slender, largely underground;
plant perennial, tuberous, 15. Conopodium,
    PIGNUT

Beside the pignut, dangling over the edge of the pool between cracks
in the blue render, is a languor of spearmint with a single yellow flower
like a star at the edge of a galaxy, shadowed by the branches of an elderberry

beneath which we buried a family tomcat wrapped in a tea towel with his head pointing homewards. I've resisted demands to cut it down, citing the pagan notion that one mustn't cut the branches of the elderberry unless one has a good intention.

And I have no intentions at all.

Last August I watched a whitethroat hanging upside down there, feasting on sprays of the elderberry's black fruit.

The Blue Slug

A blue slug, the colour of biro ink,
makes its way down the side of a rotting log
and slides past the fire I've cultivated.
Is this the month that slugs and snails change sex,
this blue a final blue of indecision?
I don't inhabit the kingdom of the slug
and am, alas, only and forever male
with worse indecisions all of my own.

The sun is setting without hesitation,
so colour and temperature reverse.
Will the White Admiral, mostly brown,
that seems to think my cabin belongs to him
and sips sweat from the bald patch on my head,
now expand and reappear as an angel,
a lord of light with a flaming sword
saying, "Welcome home, Son of Adam?"

Will the blue slug inflate into a devil,
scarlet now with twitching horns and grinning,
"Your last sin, thinking a slug is just a slug?"
The stream beside my cabin has turned dark
glistening like old Kodak negative.
The girl in the moon floats up above the pines,
a celebrity simply passing through
an occasion too trifling to stay long.

Indeed nothing happens. The White Admiral
has folded up its wings fidgeting to stillness
imitating a leaf. The blue slug
has, no doubt, inched across the slick dew
to feed on burdock or angelica.
Coolness at midnight sidles through the trees
and yet I leave the cabin door ajar
to watch the fire I made dwindle, then wink out.

At the Table

At the table under the hornbeam or ironwood or yoke tree, guardian
of homes, double-trunked from the ground up, splashed with lichen
on their northern sides, profuse with leaf and beyond the hornbeam
the main stream with beech trees on the opposite bank stabilizing a
virtual cliff, the nearest tree again a double trunk straight for sixty
feet before the first branches with leaf and ninety feet more to the
crown, the other beeches straight as well, pewter-coloured in the
forest light above the stream's rustle through which ring snakes pass,
lazy slivers of light assuring the water's purity despite the debris
from logging upstream:

at the table under the hornbeam,

at a table made from a sycamore trunk halved down the middle
slowly succumbing to years of weather, the mycelia of a rubbery
fungus and an archipelago of moss in the creases in the surface of
the table, dark green tropical islands towards which a tiny spider,
mottled like the ageing table, tacks, its legs to my squinting gaze
like oars moving rapidly, a cutter from a privateer in search of
plunder disappearing and reappearing in the swell of a sycamore sea.

Awaking a Peacock Butterfly

Almost a fragment of old-fashioned carbon paper; I relive
a forty-year old excitement of two or three copies of a poem,
fit enough for the two-fingered labour of typing on my Olivetti,
shaken out from under the original, their letters fuzzy round
the edges like tiny caterpillars in a variety of postures.

A piece of darkness oddly perpendicular resisting the temptations
of gravity to subside and lie flat, I take it up between forefinger
and thumb, carry it out of my cabin then place it in the sun where
it topples as air gusts over.
Dead, after remaining upright all winter?

Not so. Antennae and legs have unfolded. It quivers in the now
still air, shudders, fibrillates as though it might shake itself into
black dust. Solar power and whatever smidgeon of insect blood
ripples the colours of its wings like tiny counterpanes. The merest
flicker of the edges of its wings and it's off.

Then I notice Brimstone, the original 'butter fly', Hairstreak, Queen
of Spain, Speckled Wood, a large fritillary, Banded White, a Blue
and a first Camberwell Beauty's rapid linear flight between willow
and willow while above two ravens chuckle observations.
Carbon copies of each other, they will not change.

Nuptials

Two Silver-Washed Fritillaries over clumps of hairy-stemmed scabious;
the male, I assume, from its larger size, darker spots and the green
pattern on the underside of its wings like a fragment of a large scale
ordnance survey map, is mostly inert when the female flies to another
flowerhead, like all females of the species so much more versatile than
the male, which hangs from her like a piece of delicate luggage although
occasionally he stirs and then the pair seem to be one large butterfly with
slightly asymmetrical wings.

A third fritillary, another male, attempts to butt in and there is a brief
orgy of orange shot through with black and green over the pink scabious
before the mating pair ascend to continue and conclude on the leaves of a
neighbouring hazel bush and the intruder glides off.

Later I find the first male spent on the grass by my cabin.

He does not fly away when I stoop over him.

Red Admiral, White Admiral

Freshly emerged from its chrysalis, its complex eyes shiny oval
portholes, it crosses my threshold and rests on the floor of the cabin.
I wet a finger to revive it with my saliva.
A black proboscis all of a piece with its glossy thorax and abdomen
unfurls and sucks.

It looks as though just promoted from commodore to admiral, the
red bands on its wings shine like new braid on dress uniform, spick
and span for a review of the fleet with royalty to be piped aboard.

It flies off elegantly unlike the battered old warrior that circles my
head shortly afterwards its wings ragged in a combat brown and white.
Briefly it settles, heaving to on my wetted finger uncoiling a yellow
tongue to imbibe before an agitated patrol and attack.

Am I too near its bramble patch?

I flap a hand and it vanishes until I feel a disturbance in my hair.
In the glass of my cabin door I see it victorious, the enemy a prize
firmly under its legs as it splices the main-brace from the sweat on
my bald patch.

Bat Flying in Daylight

It must have been like this for those two little girls
a hundred years ago in a magical wood
through which a stream intoned arcane syllables:

a sudden erratic swoop, a hovering
above glinting water, tumbling over itself,
then off, its return immediate, quivering

in a frantic exhilaration of paper thin wings
through which the sun poured so the fairy caught fire
yet did not burn. Instead it seemed to be beckoning.

I watched it flicker away again then glide
close to the tarry surface of a telephone pole
its claws scraping purchase, its head to one side

attempting to make sense out of the daylight air
through birdsong and insect rustle, its own soundings
beyond my hearing crying, "Where, where? Where, where?"

Dormouse

It woke me up,
first tipping a coffee cup
over in its saucer
while slipping through
the barred window in the kitchen,
next flipping over
a wooden herb pot
with 'DILL' scored
in black lettering
on its way from windowsill
to the shelf above the hotplate
dislodging a white jar that fell
with a hiss and a crash
as rice poured out
and the jar itself bounced
but didn't shatter.

I clicked on the light
whose flicker caught it
in the act perched
on the edge of the sink, crouched
over a side plate filching
a bread crust I'd left.
Unflustered, it blinked at me,
tail a grey five-inch feather duster,
ears twitching back and forth,
eyes all black inquiring pupil
as if saying
"You did leave it,
so if I may,"
before sidestepping away
down off the draining board
by means of the handle
of the door of the cupboard

under the sink, not in fright,
but defter through caution
than before, crust in its mouth,
to a spot out of sight
where it must have fed
after I'd clicked off the light
and gone back to bed.

A Fear of Storms

Yesterday it poured and will pour again,
shortly if the heavy cloud cover
is to be believed. The last drummed down blessings
lie inert, transparent yet almost alive
like liquid serpents between ruts in the grass.

Lightning rips the horizon softly,
a tear with threads and stitches of brilliance
zig-zagging above into nothingness
and below into the hills with a hiss
as though a silk dress parted at the seams.

An intimation of new rain descends
in single privileged drops exploding,
flickering into beads on purple dead nettle,
wood anemone, lungwort, yellow rattle,
honesty, Star of Bethlehem, archangel;

descends on your face, but does not break
rolling down with forest vowels of patter,
whisper, gossip, insinuation, chatter,
diatribe, tirade of flash and noise,
the illumination, the voice that destroys.

Web

The storm dawdles behind the ridge
that hides the south from me,
a glower above beech and spruce
with crude webs of lightning
that form, fizz and fray while rain bangs
a passionate measure
on the panels roofing my deck.

Almost-invisibilities
attach a web to the pillars
that keep roof and gutter over me.
I've counted twenty-eight
divisions radiating out,
a polygon of spit,
glinting as lightning flickers,

whose threads have enough give and take
to hold the shaking web
and the spider at its centre.
I think thought is like this,
then understand it isn't thought
but what comes after thought
begins and before thought has done:

stillness, impulse, a rapid act
which doesn't shift the spider
even though wind gusts exaggerate
the web this way and that.
How can a spider know weather
from individual
struggles of lacewing, midge or moth?

Can the spider and its web survive?
All night the rain pelts down
as I lie awake recalling
your goodbye, lips on mine,
hardly a kiss, hardly a thought.
By morning it seems, save
for a torn edge, the web has held.

Z

Between us beams of sunlight slant
hazy with dust but shapely
like the long legs of Zlatica
in sheer stockings glinting as she walks.

The sunlight vanishes in cloud
as the golden girl, Zlatica,
her breasts small and high and firm,
the golden apples of the sun,

walks ahead of me to the tower
where she will talk about Great Works
finished by another. Zlatica,
who I might have claimed for myself

had the aspects, the elements,
the condition of my soul been right
in this country where Zlatica
walks and shakes her golden head.

Acknowledgements

Some of these poems have appeared in print and electronic magazines including *The Bow-Wow Shop, Café Poetry Review, Ink Sweat and Tears, Magma, Peony Moon, Poetry and Places, Poetry Out Loud (POL), Poetry Review, Qualm, Sahitto, Screech Owl, Stand.*

'Whodunnit' was published in George Hitchcock's legendary *Kayak* magazine in 1976. 'Nightowl' was broadcast in the *Living Poet* series in September 1985 on Radio 3 in a thirty-minute programme on my work called *In the Country of Rumour* compiled by Roberta Berke and produced by the late Piers Plowright. A number of these poems have been translated into Serbian and Slovak and the translations published and, in Slovakia, broadcast on Radio Devin. I'm grateful to my Serbian translators, the poets Ivana Milankov and Ivanka Radmanović and my Slovak translators, Ján Gavura, Joe Palaščák and Michal Tallo. In Serbia translations of these poems have been published in the literary magazines *Stremljenja* and *Stig* and in a number of anthologies published by the Association of Serbian Writers for their International Meeting of Writers in Belgrade between 2003 and 2019. In Slovakia translation of poems in this collection have appeared in the literary magazines *Fraktal* and *Vertigo*. A group of poems was translated for the Novotar Festival in Bratislava in 2019.

'Pure Mathematics' received a Runners-up Prize in the very last Peterloo Competition in 2003.

'Rosa Canina' was long-listed and was published in the anthology, *Tremble*, for the University of Canberra's Vice-Chancellor's International Poetry Prize in 2016.

'The End of the Affair' was long-listed and was published in the anthology, *Irises*, for the University of Canberra's Vice-Chancellor's International Poetry Prize in 2017.

'Girls, Dogs and Depleted Uranium' was long-listed and was published in the anthology, *Signs*, for the University of Canberra's Vice-Chancellor's International Poetry Prize in 2018.